CROSSING TH

*Practical and Spiritual Guidance
on Death and Dying
Based on the Work of Rudolf Steiner*

*Nicholas Wijnberg
and Philip Martyn*

TEMPLE LODGE

Temple Lodge Publishing
Hillside House, The Square
Forest Row, RH18 5ES

www.templelodge.com

Published by Temple Lodge 2003

A catalogue record for this book is available from the British Library

ISBN 1 902636 42 2

Cover art by Anne Stockton, layout by Andrew Morgan
Typeset by DP Photosetting, Aylesbury, Bucks.
Printed and bound by Cromwell Press Limited, Trowbridge, Wilts.

CONTENTS

All things alive throughout the universe
Live only by bringing forth within them
The seed of a new life
So too the soul of man is given up
To ageing and to death
Only that deathless he may ripen
To ever newly resurrected life

Rudolf Steiner

PREFACE

This short book offers assistance to those accompanying someone through the process of dying, or making funeral and related arrangements for someone who has died. Written from the standpoint of anthroposophy and the Christian Community,[1] the first section of this book deals with Rudolf Steiner's approach to funerals and was inspired by the publication in Stuttgart of a similar book by Michael Debus and Gunhild Kačer for local Anthroposophical Society members. We have made use of their research and gratefully acknowledge their work. This book continues with a description of the period leading up to death, suggesting ways of coping at this time and afterwards. Then follow sections that examine different circumstances of death and our continuing relation to the departed soul. Finally there is a practical section which helps with such matters as laying out the body, legal requirements and wills.

The authors gratefully acknowledge the insights, guidance and help gained from Rudolf Steiner, anthroposophy and the religious life of the Christian Community.

---

[1] For more information, see further reading list, and/or contact your local Christian Community congregation. If there is no local congregation in your area, contact: The Christian Community, Hartfield Road, School Lane, Forest Row, East Sussex RH18 5DZ UK.
(*Technical note:* Within the Christian Community it is conventional to capitalize the 't' of the definite article, i.e. '*The* Christian Community'. In this book, for reasons of the publisher's house style, a lower case 't' has been adopted throughout.)

1

THE MEANING OF DEATH

Death is an inevitable reality for all of us. From an earthly perspective we may feel it to be a final ending, but a spiritual point of view can show it in a different light: not merely an end but also a mighty moment of transition: a threshold rather than an impenetrable barrier, a gateway to a non-earthly form of existence with its own non-earthly laws.

We can only comprehend this transition through insight into the nature of the human being. As well as a mortal physical body, we also have the life body (etheric), the soul (astral) and the eternal spirit or 'I' — which together constitute our fourfold nature.[1] Each of these four interpenetrating aspects has its own laws and possibilities: our whole being is a marvellously wise and complex interaction of all four levels. Later we will examine what happens to each of these four bodies at death.

When faced with the death of someone close to us, our thoughts easily tend in one or another direction: either emphasizing our loss and mourning over the dead body, thus to some extent ignoring spirit reality; or instead seeing this spirit reality as all-important, and considering the reality of the body — which during life was permeated by the living spirit and has thus become spiritualized substance — to be of little or no importance.

We believe both aspects to be very important. As

authors our aim is to help create an awareness of how we can prepare for and support the transition of death through our understanding and our actions. To do justice to this reality we need to keep in mind the complex physical-spiritual nature of man as a fourfold being.

Broadly our theme can be divided into the following five stages:

I. In biological terms the whole span of our life from birth onwards is orientated towards death. Death processes are at work (though to a lesser degree in childhood) from our first breath of air. This first stage represents a journey of exploration into life, everything that happens in terms of our experiences and choice of lifestyles, and where we choose to devote our energies: whether we live a completely outward life, a very inward one or a balance of the two. Some events and experiences really bring home to us our mortal nature, the fact that we will die one day.

In cultivating a more inward sense of things we may become increasingly aware of the spiritual consequences of the way we lead our life. A reminder of this reality is given in the Christian Community's funeral service which expresses that we are 'beholden to the spirit' for all our thoughts, words and deeds.

In material terms, preparing for death includes making arrangements for what should happen to our earthly belongings. Questions about funeral arrangements, though, also have an important aspect of inner preparation. The kind of funeral chosen will actually be significant in assisting the transition which takes place at death. Clear communication with those who will be involved with the funeral can help.

2. A second stage may be seen in the phase immediately preceding death. Here circumstances tend to be very individual. Death may come very suddenly and unexpectedly, or may be prepared through a prolonged period of illness, possibly also involving life-support machines; or perhaps it will occur peacefully at home.

   In most of these situations — sometimes, as subtle premonition, even in a case of what appears to be sudden death — the person who dies or those close to him* will have a heightened awareness of the approaching threshold of death.

   Anxieties might arise, deeper questions may need addressing, and difficulties will need to be resolved. All those involved will require sensitivity. At this stage religious or spiritual support from a priest and friends may be just as important as medical treatment.

3. After lifelong preparation and (in most cases) a shorter, more intense last phase of preparation for death, the actual moment of death seals the life we have led with a final conclusion. At this third stage we can witness a unique, awe-filled moment of the spirit's victory over matter: a moment that can never be fully anticipated and that to some degree always takes us by surprise. From this moment onwards the response of friends and family as well as the wider community will come to expression.

4. The three days immediately after death form the fourth stage. This is a precious and holy time of transition from the earthly world into the world of spirit. In accompanying this process we need to strive for heightened awareness and the ability to act with clarity of purpose, despite our feelings of shock and grief. By informing the priest immediately, we enable him to accompany the soul and make the most appropriate funeral preparations.

5. After three days a further transition occurs and the fifth stage begins. This is the time when the funeral can be held. With the dissolution of the etheric body and its return to the realm of life forces, the deceased person's soul and spirit loosens its links with the physical body, and a new step on the journey into the world of spirit takes place. The continuing process of remembering and accompanying the deceased person now begins. In Chapter 7 this fifth stage will be described in more detail.

2

THE CHRISTIAN COMMUNITY FUNERAL SERVICE AND THE ANTHROPOSOPHICAL MOVEMENT

We can best help and guide the transition from physical to spiritual existence at death when our earthly consciousness and way of dealing with the situation corresponds as much as possible to what the person who has died experiences in the spiritual world.

Living with the so-called dead, carrying them in our consciousness along their spiritual path, is an inherent part of a truly spiritual approach to life. In maintaining and nurturing this connection beyond the threshold of death we not only help and support departed souls, but also enable these souls to more easily help and inspire the living. The funeral service, particularly the Christian Community funeral service given by Rudolf Steiner, is a major contribution towards fulfilling this aim. This service can be seen as inaugurating a new way of relating to the person who has just died.

This relating and communicating may become 'ever more holy for us', because 'what they (the dead) can give to us now from the other world is more precious for them than what they could give to us on the physical plane'.[1]

Such insight shows that the practical way we deal with a death will be of great importance! 'Although it may sound strange,' says Steiner, ' whether a funeral is correctly or incorrectly conducted is far more important for human social existence than a local council or Parliament decision'.[2]

A deeper understanding of what a funeral really involves may be found through exploring Rudolf Steiner's approach to this theme and the guidance he has given us about it. On many occasions he was asked to officiate at funerals, but always refused, seeing this as the task of a priest or minister. He never performed any ritual or liturgy in such situations. Rudolf Steiner's contribution at funerals was always restricted to giving an address, and wherever possible he would ask a church minister to officiate.

A new development in the history of the Christian Community funeral service arose through the funeral of Marie Hahn. Dr Steiner made it a condition that he would only give an address at the funeral if a minister conducted the service preceding his address. The deceased and her husband, Rudolf Hahn, had lost all connection with their own church. For this reason Rudolf Steiner approached Rev. Hugo Schuster and asked him to conduct the funeral service.

Rev. Hugo Schuster was a priest, anthroposophist and personal pupil of Rudolf Steiner. The Old Catholic Church in which he had been ordained, and which separated from the Catholic Church in 1870, was formed of clergy opposed to the doctrine of the infallibility of the Pope, proclaimed by the first Vatican Council of 1869/70. At this funeral which took place on 22 September 1918, Rudolf Steiner began his address with the following words: 'After the priestly word has lead the soul whom we love from the visible to the invisible world...'[3]

Rudolf Hahn, the widower, reported however that after the funeral Rudolf Steiner stated that this Old Catholic Church ritual was 'simply too feeble' and that 'something new and more appropriate would have to be found'.

As an initiate, Rudolf Steiner was able to receive the new funeral service from the spiritual world, and entrusted it to Hugo Schuster as an ordained minister. This new funeral service was celebrated for the first time on 14 January 1919, at Marie Leyh's funeral in Arlesheim. On this historically important occasion Rudolf Steiner gave an address which began with the following words: 'After the consecrated word of the priest has resounded, which should guide the soul of our dear Mrs Leyh into the heights of spirit realms...'[4]

On two further occasions, 12 May 1920 for Johanna Peelen, and 27 October 1920 for Caroline Wilhelm, the new funeral service was celebrated by Rev. Hugo Schuster in the presence of Rudolf Steiner. On both occasions Rudolf Steiner gave an address at the end of the service.

At the end of 1921 Hugo Schuster took early retirement from the Old Catholic Church due to ill health. The new funeral service was then entrusted to the Christian Community and became part of the body of sacraments and liturgy of this 'Movement for Religious Renewal' when it was founded in September 1922 in Dornach, Switzerland, with the help of Rudolf Steiner.

In preparing for the founding of the Christian

Community, Rudolf Steiner spoke about the funeral service to future priests in October 1921, referring to it as a 'ritual which I know from my direct observation has proven itself in practice'.[5]

He then spoke about how this new funeral service, which had until then been entrusted to Hugo Schuster, really does contain spiritual deeds which are best able to guide the deceased soul's existence from the 'world of physical being into the world of spiritual existence'.[6]

In referring to the new funeral service, therefore, Rudolf Steiner was now able to describe how the soul is led not only 'from the visible into the invisible world', but 'into the world of spiritual existence' and into the 'heights of spirit realms'. This was a fundamentally new step in the development of Christian ritual and liturgy: the human being is now addressed as a being of body, soul and spirit, rather than one only of body and soul.

This major development took place after almost a thousand years of denial of the human being's full spiritual reality. At the Eighth Ecumenical Council at Constantinople in 869, the Church Fathers declared that we consist only of body and soul, and that the spirit can only be reached through the mediation of the Church. From that time, doctrinally speaking, the spiritual nature of the human being was 'abolished'. This dogma denied the possibility of finding truth as a free human being independently of the Church's external authority.

But since the beginning of the last century, spiritual science (anthroposophy) has once more enabled us to see ourselves as beings of body, soul and spirit. At the same time this opens up for us the possibility of independent access to realms of divine spirit and universal truth. This is reflected also in the new funeral service which not only leads the soul into the 'calm of soul existence' but guides and helps the spirit to enter into the 'light of the spirit world'.

After the founding of the Christian Community, Rudolf Steiner was present and gave an address at three funerals conducted by priests of this recently-formed Movement for Religious Renewal. The first occasion was the funeral of Elisabeth Maier, celebrated by Gertrud Spoerri on 29 March 1923, and the second that of Hermann Linde, celebrated by Friedrich Doldinger on 29 June 1923.

Two weeks after the latter funeral Rudolf Steiner met again with the priests of the Christian Community in Stuttgart, and spoke about how 'Ritual in the way in which it is intended to work within this religious movement is the direct language of the spiritual world, brought down into earthly form; taking part in the ritual is therefore something entirely positive.'[7] He then went on to state clearly how he envisaged that the Christian Community and the anthroposophical movement would work together in regard to funerals:

> Now, anthroposophists claim that certain advanced persons have no need of the ritual. This question could actually not arise at all if people had the right attitude. I simply cannot conceive on what grounds it could arise. Imagine a funeral is to take place now. Then, quite obviously, the religious community is called upon to carry out the ritual aspect.

And likewise, through the Act of Consecration of Man it is called upon to address the whole human being—and certainly not merely with the intention that it is something temporary which one day will have to be replaced by something else. It is something eternal, in so far as anything on the earth can be called eternal.

On occasions when social relationships are to be consecrated through the ritual I shall never again do anything unless a representative of our religious movement is also involved. At funerals I shall no longer speak unless a priest is also present. The ritual has to be carried out. In this way, a right judgement must gradually be formed. When people debate and discuss, they misunderstand each other, but facts speak for themselves.[8]

The third and final occasion when Rudolf Steiner gave an address at a Christian Community funeral was at the funeral of Edith Maryon, celebrated by Friedrich Dol-dinger on 6 May 1924.

When Edith Maryon died in Dornach on 2 May 1924, Rudolf Steiner personally requested the funeral service of the Christian Community. The following telegram was sent to Rev. Doldinger: 'Would you be able to come here on Tuesday at 11 o'clock for the cremation of Edith Maryon?—Rudolf Steiner.'

Rudolf Steiner made his last direct reference to the Christian Community funeral service on 27 June 1924. Here he spoke of ritual as something which cannot be 'thought out' but which must be an expression of spiritual processes and realities. In this context he went on to speak about the funeral ritual as 'a small part of the ritual life as it has established itself within the Movement for Religious Renewal and which obviously, my dear friends, most of you know is a funeral ritual established in the sense of our Christian Community'.[9]

Less than a year later the Christian Community funeral service was celebrated for Rudolf Steiner himself. Friedrich Rittelmeyer held the service at the request of Marie Steiner. The first part of the ritual took place in the evening of 2 April 1925 in the Schreinerei (joinery workshop) at the Goetheanum in Dornach. The second part took place the next day, at Basle crematorium.

We can see, therefore, the great importance Rudolf Steiner placed on the new funeral ritual as a way of assisting departed souls into the spiritual world.

3

PREPARING FOR DEATH

We experience tremendous joy at the birth of a child. With the first breath of air the tiny child takes hold of an earthly body, and this becomes the home of a being which has descended from the cosmic universe to participate in life on earth. We give all our love and help to make the new arrival feel at home in its body and surroundings.

Separated by a lifetime from the moment of first breath is that of breathing out the last breath of air here on earth, when we leave our earthly body again and return to the world we came from at birth. This moment too is a profound transition.

That we find ourselves in an altered state of consciousness while asleep is a fact generally accepted. Sleep is a state of being where we do not have all our faculties at our disposal: our spirit and soul, which enable us to have consciousness and experience the world around us, detach from our physical and life bodies during sleep. Death can be seen as a further, final stage in this process of separating from our physical bodies, when not only our spirit and soul but also the life or etheric body withdraws, so that our life functions cannot continue.

In the same way that the day of our birth cannot be precisely calculated, we are likewise unable to determine the time of our death. It always comes as a surprise; and yet, by its very nature, despite perhaps difficult outer circumstances, death belongs to life as much as sleep does. Accepting it as such, rather than seeking to avoid it at all costs, enables us to help and accompany the departed soul in the most beneficial way. Although the law in Britain, for instance, insists on a cause being cited for every death that occurs, we do not have to see death primarily as having an outer cause, even when directly resulting from illness.

It is the prevalence of materialistic thinking which leads us to avoid and reject suffering and death: for such thinking can find in them no meaning or sense, but only failure and defeat.

In contrast, spiritual traditions which acknowledge further realms of being beyond the material can also accept death as a step on the journey to other, deeper, further life. In Christianity, death is given new reality through the fact that Christ connects and unites the divine with all that belongs to the sense perceptible world, all that belongs to our humanity. Christ's death and resurrection embrace our humanity and give it full expression and potential.

In imbuing ourselves with the essence of Christianity we find a reality within our mortal existence which prepares us for deathless life beyond the gates of death. In dying, our 'I' or true being transcends into the world of spirit, into the divine world, the realms of God. We may view the entire span of our life as an ongoing preparation for this moment. The higher, deathless, life can be experienced particularly when we enter in meditation and prayer into the quiet of our 'inner room', the chamber of our heart.[1] When our bodies come to rest in meditation, our eyes close, our hands are folded, we can begin to familiarize ourselves with the world we will meet in death. Spiritual concepts and thoughts, gained for instance through studying anthroposophy, help too in preparing us for the realm beyond the threshold of death.

When we visit a foreign country, we find ourselves much better able to find our way about if we have done some homework in advance. Maps and travel guides help us to become more familiar with various aspects of this country, such as geography and language.

Likewise, in immersing ourselves in spiritual science we can prepare ourselves for the journey to the spiritual realm beyond the threshold of death. Through inner preparation, through understanding of spiritual matters which we have gained while on earth, we can more easily adjust to our new form of existence after death, with its own spiritual laws.

Facing death

Even though we may have lived with thoughts and concepts about the reality of life beyond death, when nearing this threshold in our own lives we stand nonetheless before a new and not fully comprehensible experience.

Coming to terms with this can naturally evoke fear and uncertainty. Yet we can take certain conscious steps in the midst of life that help overcome taboos and enable us to face the existential reality of our own death. We may consider questions such as what will happen to our earthly possessions when we have passed on (or even before death) and how our deeper, eternal impulses will continue after death. Making a will helps not only order the distribution of our earthly possessions after we die, but—as an expression of our *will*—enables us to seek purpose and meaning in deeper impulses with which we will remain connected after death.

The funeral service is of great significance in supporting and guiding the transition from the earthly world to that of the spirit. Clearly expressing one's wishes helps avoid unclarity and possible misunderstandings at the time of death. Those who are not members of the Christian Community may still wish to have the Christian Community funeral service; and if so, it is of great importance to take up contact with a priest of the nearest Christian Community congregation in order to communicate such a wish. Membership of the Christian Community is not a requirement in order to receive a Christian Community funeral. However, for inner, esoteric reasons, personal contact before death would be of great significance in enabling the best possible preparation for the funeral service.

In order for 'social relationships to be consecrated through the ritual', communication during lifetime is of paramount importance, not least because, at the funeral service, the priest describes the biography of the person who has died; so it is of tremendous help if the priest can experience the person before death.

The challenge of illness

Illness can often be experienced as a time of heightened awareness. Precisely in situations where we experience dysfunction and pain in our physical body, we may also become more aware of our soul and spirit nature. Reflecting on our life and questioning its significance and meaning may well be part of the process. The more serious the illness the more intense this process will be.

Illness — terminal illness included — is a challenge for us to confront and work with. Even where an illness leads to death we can speak of coming to terms with the illness and, to a greater or lesser degree, of mastering it in an inner sense.

We can see that illness is not only a medical question but also something which equally addresses the soul and spiritual nature of the human being, requiring accompaniment and support.

How illness is dealt with is always very individual and will depend on individual destiny, and such factors as how we have led our life up to this point. The type of illness will also present its own typical picture. General patterns can often be recognized in the phases of an illness and in the particular difficulties but also possibilities which the illness in question presents.

In accompanying a seriously ill person we enter on an inner path. Wrestling with the situation, despair and denial, but also acceptance and transformation, may all be experienced along the way.

Those who accompany a sick person in this way need to find inner calm and a sense of divine purpose in order to be able to help the patient find certainty and feel supported. Above all, listening and compassion will be called for. It may often be impossible for the sick person to verbalize real inner needs and concerns — not surprising since this is often no different in ordinary healthy life! Those who attend and accompany the sick person will need to listen to what is trying to come to expression behind the words, or perhaps in silence.

A sick person may need support for the inner health and peace of soul, and will often respond strongly to surrounding sense impressions. It may for instance be helpful to adjust the amount of (preferably natural) light in the room. Pictures and flowers may help raise a patient's spirits.

Reading from the gospels and praying is a powerful food for the soul and spirit, though of course this should not be forced on anyone. Familiar passages from the gospels can give strength and spiritual nourishment. Content related to particular seasons in the Christian cycle of the year may be relevant too. In very difficult phases of the illness, and in the period immediately after death, chapters 14–17 of the Gospel of St. John are of great benefit.

These chapters of the Bible form what is known as the 'farewell discourses' spoken by Jesus on Maundy Thursday, immediately before the events leading to his own death on Good Friday. These chapters can be experienced as a profound prayer by Christ to the Father God on behalf of needy humanity.

Speaking the Lord's Prayer for the patient can provide

daily spiritual sustenance. Reciting of Psalms (e.g. Psalm 23) and verses brings strength and comfort too.

In looking back on life there may well be issues which still need to be resolved, or encounters which can still take place. It has often been observed that terminally ill patients await a particular event or encounter before crossing over the threshold of death. In some instances it appears miraculous that the dying person holds on until a certain visitor arrives. In other situations a dying person may choose a brief moment when alone in her room to cross over into the other world. The time of death however is known to higher, spiritual beings, and depends also on planetary configurations of the constellations, as a 'gateway' to the spirit's future growth.

A priest consulted in situations of severe illness will be able to give individual advice and support. The patient can gain great benefit from having both doctor and priest to accompany the process which may lead to death.

The last anointing

Death is often anticipated, through circumstances of chronic illness or where certain symptoms of old age become more noticeable. In such situations the priest may be asked to assist. Help can be given through the last anointing, one of the seven sacraments. Before proceeding with the last anointing, certain factors should be taken into consideration.

It will be helpful to consider the relationship which

the dying person has to religion and the sacramental life. In some instances (for example, if the dying person is unconscious) a request for last anointing may come from someone else. In such circumstances a conversation is needed to assess the situation and try to ascertain whether this is appropriate, and in accord with the dying person's wishes.

The last anointing is a sacrament whose archetype consists of three different parts:

– The sacramental consultation
– Communion for the sick
– The anointing itself

The first two stages may take place at an earlier stage in the illness, or may be included in a combined, three-part ceremony.

The sacramental consultation
The first of these three stages, the sacramental consultation, offers a sacred space in which the dying person can reflect on her destiny, and through which events of her life can be brought to consciousness before the divine world. In this sacramental act preparation is given for meeting more consciously and openly what every soul meets after death: acknowledgement before the divine world of our life with all its joys and sorrows, failures and successes. By its very nature the sacramental consultation requires the dying person to be still conscious and, even if only to a limited extent, able to enter into a conversation.

Communion for the sick

If the dying person has in some way lived with the healing process of the sacraments, at the threshold of death communion may be one of the last earthly substances taken in. Healing is given in the transubstantiated bread and wine. The karma of the dying person is brought into intimate relationship with consecrated substances of the earth, with substances penetrated with the higher life-giving power of Christ. For the communion service for the sick, the physical ability to receive and digest the consecrated substances of bread and wine would be necessary.

Anointing

As part of the anointing sacrament itself, a rendering of the 17th Chapter of the Gospel of St John is spoken. This profound passage with its deep, mantric quality precedes the anointing which then takes place with consecrated oil. Oil, in this case olive oil, bears the strongest forces of the sun within the plant kingdom. Just as oil has the possibility of making translucent (this can be observed by holding greased paper up to the light), so too this sacrament acts like a window, opening up the destiny situation of the dying person, and prepares the soul to behold the spirit. Sacramental words are spoken and three crosses are made on the forehead with the consecrated oil: one cross above each eyebrow and one cross in the centre of the forehead. The crosses of Golgotha, (which means 'place of the skull') are inscribed on the skull of the dying person. The forthcoming moment of death is brought into an inner relationship with Christ's death on the hill of Golgotha and the overcoming of death. The anointing itself is still possible even when the dying person is no longer conscious, although it may not be possible to carry out the first two stages.

The last anointing should be administered at an advanced stage in the illness, close to the threshold of death. Priest and doctor will ideally be able to work together in order to determine the appropriate moment for this sacrament.

Through the last anointing, the dying person's destiny is given over into the hands of the divine world. The transition to death may often come quickly, but the dying person may also, however, rally and return to full health. In such cases anointing can be repeated whenever the person concerned again approaches the threshold of death at a later stage of life.

4

THE MOMENT OF DEATH AND THE DAYS IMMEDIATELY AFTER

At the moment of death we experience the great victory of spirit over matter. For those left behind, however, this can be a moment of great loss. Rudolf Steiner gives the following description of the moment of death:

> The nature of the experience of the moment of death is such that it leaves impressions of deepest impact for the entire life between death and a new birth. Of all experiences this is most clearly remembered, and remains continually present, though in a different way from how this is perceived from the earthly perspective. From our perspective death appears as disintegration, as something towards which we feel fear and horror. From the other side however, death appears as the brightest beginning of spiritual life, as something which radiates sun-like over the entire life between death and new birth. It is something which warms our souls most in life after death, something which we always look back to with deepest sympathy. This is the moment of death. If we want to express it in earthly words we would have to say: The highest delight, the most beautiful reality in life between death and a new birth is the moment of death as it is experienced from beyond the threshold.[1]

It can help the bereaved to approach the person who has just crossed the threshold in the awareness that something mighty and holy is taking place for him. Praying the Lord's Prayer could be an appropriate response to the situation, before doing anything else or thinking of more practical considerations.

The deceased person enters a realm where he calmly and objectively views his life from a higher perspective. For a period of 3 days he is surrounded by what is known as the 'life panorama'. All of his life unfurls before him in a mighty tableau, through the loosening of the etheric body—the bearer of memory—from the physical.

The priest and the doctor should be informed as soon as possible after the moment of death, though if the death takes place at night it may be advisable in some cases to wait until morning before informing them. You should usually notify priest and doctor before calling in the undertaker. The priest may be able to advise on funeral arrangements, and on what may be appropriate to request from the undertaker. In some situations relatives may wish to arrange the funeral without engaging the services of an undertaker.

The laying out

During the first three days after death an intimate relationship exists between the deceased person and his body. Wherever possible, it is of profound support to the deceased to lay out his body for the duration of this time.

Legal considerations may have to be taken into account, particularly if the coroner is involved. Uncertainties may also arise with regard to various practical matters. Qualified advice will often be needed. The priest, local funeral support group, or other individuals may be able to help clarify any uncertainties about what is appropriate and what is really legally or practically necessary in any situation. The aim should always be, however, whenever possible, for laying out to take place over the first three days. It is worth recalling that Jesus Christ lay in the grave for three days, between the crucifixion and the resurrection; and that in this period He descended to the underworld — or lower astral world — where human souls were trapped after death, thus liberating humanity and making our upward evolution possible once more.[2]

After human death an intimate and precious relationship exists between the physical body and the spirit. As we mentioned, the etheric body or body of life-forces slowly withdraws from the physical body. This slow withdrawal of the etheric body results in the memory being freed so that all the deeds and events of our life surround us in a mighty panorama for about three days.

The physical body, which has been a temple for the indwelling eternal 'I' or spirit during life now becomes apparent to the soul as a precious reality for the earth and for humanity. So much will have been suffered and worked through, sacrificed and transformed during the course of life, while the body was penetrated by the individual who has died. The close, intimate connection with the physical body now broadens into something purely objective for the person who has died, and also for those left behind.

A chapel of rest specially dedicated for laying out the dead will provide a worthy place for the body to lie for three days. If none is available, the room where the person has died may also offer a good possibility for laying out. The room needs to be kept cool throughout this time. Depending on the season it may help to draw the curtains. Likewise a portable air-conditioner, or dry ice, may be used to help keep the temperature down.

Embalming, which is often provided as a service by undertakers, is not advisable. Embalming disturbs the natural process of the etheric body's withdrawal from the physical body.

A relatively simple procedure can be followed in order to prepare the body for the laying out and the final farewell (see 'Practical Aspects'). This preparation may be done by the undertaker; or people close to the deceased may wish to administer these last offices themselves. Dressing the deceased person in a white shroud, blouse or similar, can always be experienced as giving festive and dignified expression to what is taking place. Candles can be placed left and right of the body, near the head. The gentle light of the candles can illuminate the countenance.

Cut flowers, a symbol of offering, are a wonderful gesture. Some flowers can be left to wilt — for instance by placing them around the body. The process which takes place in the wilting of flowers echoes the similar process taking place in the body, strongly emphasizing the sphere of the liberated life forces.

For those accompanying the process this can be a
quiet time of keeping watch or 'waking'. When possible,
a steady, alternating presence of friends may enable the
deceased person to be accompanied throughout this
time. There is however no absolute necessity for this.
Our support during these three days is of a very subtle
but profound nature. We can attempt through our presence, our thoughts and our prayers, to enter into the
objective realm in which the deceased person dwells.
Reading from the Gospels — the Gospel of St. John can be
particularly recommended — will help us enter into this
realm of pure etheric life in which the departed one now
dwells.

Speaking verses or reading content from the works of
Rudolf Steiner would not be appropriate at this time.[3]
Such wonderful, meaningful ways of accompanying the
dead have their right place after the funeral has taken
place, when a further step is taken by the deceased:
when the actual spiritual journey into life after death
really begins. Formal gatherings and memorial meetings
likewise have a much more heightened and significant
effect if they take place after the funeral.

Burial or cremation?

Burial and cremation both serve the purpose of handing
over the physical body, of returning it to the elements of
the earth. As such one can say that both these methods
fulfil this. There may be many different reasons for
choosing one or the other.

While the ultimate effect of both burial and cremation is practically the same, the essential difference is in the time needed for the process, cremation obviously being a far quicker process.

Rudolf Steiner particularly advised against cremation in the case of suicide. In this case the deceased person is helped if the physical body, left in such a sudden and difficult way, is allowed to dissolve and return to the earth slowly.

Rudolf Steiner also suggested that the souls of those who die suddenly (in an accident or catastrophe) may continue to experience a strong connection with the physical body for some time.[4] In such circumstances, therefore, consideration could be given to whether burial might be more appropriate.

When death takes place at a young age such questions can remain open. Each case will need to be considered individually; and it may well be worth discussing this with the priest if there is any doubt.

The two parts of the funeral service

The Christian Community funeral service consists of two separate ceremonies, which usually take place separately, but they can also be conducted together as a two-part ceremony.

The first of these ceremonies is generally known as 'The first part of the funeral service', but could also be called the 'Departing Blessing'. The spiritual task of this ceremony is to accompany and support the departed soul in the transition which takes place after three days. This is when the process of loosening and withdrawal of the forces of life comes to completion. This first part of the funeral is usually held where the body has been laid out for three days. Generally the coffin will be open for this short ceremony. After the service has ended, the time has come to close the coffin. In order to ensure that this service takes place at the right and meaningful time, three days after death, it is essential to make arrangements for it as soon as possible after death has occurred.

In the second part of the funeral service, spiritual support and blessing is given for the handing over of the physical remains to the elements. The journey of the departed soul into the spiritual world now begins, and the ritual gives guidance and support for this process of transition. The closed coffin will have left the more intimate situation where the laying out took place. The second part of the funeral service is usually held at the graveside, at the crematorium or in a church. Attendance of all friends, family and acquaintances will give this event its context and reality. The bereaved can find comfort, while the departed soul receives the love and prayers of those gathered for this event.

If it is not possible or appropriate to hold the funeral according to Christian Community rites, it is still important for there to be a proper funeral service of some kind, based on some religious tradition. All funeral services have the task of assisting the soul into the spiritual world, which they do more or less well depending on the spiritual efficacy of the ritual followed. Any funeral is better than no funeral, and a great deal of assistance can still be rendered to the departed soul by following the pre- and post-funeral suggestions contained in this book.

5

THE PERIOD AFTER THE FUNERAL

When we die our consciousness is not extinguished but starts to undergo radical transformation because we no longer have the physical body.

This can be a real shock, because we may not immediately realize that we are dead. It is such things as seeing the body from outside and realizing that people are not reacting to us which makes that clear. Orientation in this new realm is a major challenge and the departed soul is assisted in the transition into the spiritual world through all the events leading up to and including the funeral service. Although we have the help of spiritual beings, it makes a big difference if we also have the help of those on earth. These are the people to whom we are most closely connected and who love us. To take a simple analogy, it is the difference between going to hospital alone, on a rainy day, for a major operation, or being taken there by a good friend who keeps us company.

As already explained, in the three or four days after our death the etheric body dissolves and we start losing the feeling of gravity. The period during which our etheric body dissolves, releasing the mighty memory tableau, is one of elation for the departed soul. Since the soul is absorbed in this experience, it is not ideal to hold a memorial meeting at this time. Once the etheric body has dissolved, when the soul really starts meeting a new reality, and the spiritual journey through the planetary spheres begins, the memorial service and memorial meeting should be held; and then too one may start using the specific verses for the dead given by Rudolf Steiner.

So memorials are important because when we think with warmth of heart of someone who has died, this is like a light for them which shows them the way and reassures them — all the more so when these feelings are carried by uplifting music or singing.

The memorial service

Many religious traditions have within their sacramental sphere the possibility of uniting with and supporting the departed soul through memorial services. Within the Christian Community, the memorial service is in the form of a communion service or mass, the Act of Consecration of Man, celebrated for the departed soul. This service is always held on a Saturday, which is the day of the dead. Ideally it is held on the first Saturday after the funeral, but otherwise as soon as it is possible.

The memorial service on a Saturday is a reminder of the Easter mood of Holy Week, it being on Easter Saturday that Christ descended into hell, the realm of death, and through his deed became the 'helper of the souls of the dead'.[1] The gospel reading from the 16th chapter of St. Mark proclaims the resurrection, and through this reading and the prayers of the service we experience how the grave, which the altar symbolizes, becomes a doorway to the meeting with Christ, who overcame death after three days.

While experiencing the loss of our departed friend we can support the soul who has passed on by participating in the inner path, reflected in the memorial service, that begins at the moment of death and then leads the departing soul up into the heights of the Father God through Christ.

The funeral service builds a bridge of transition on which the soul enters into a new phase in the journey into life after death. In this new form of existence, adjustment and orientation are still needed. The memorial service helps the departed soul find this orientation and light. In receiving communion the congregation and the bereaved enter into an intimate connection with the sphere in which the departed soul now lives. It is at this juncture, directly after communion has been shared, that a prayer specially dedicated to the departed soul is spoken. Christ, the awakener of the dead is called upon to lead and guide the soul into the realm of deathless life.

The memorial meeting

After the memorial service, while all the friends are gathered, or at any other time after the funeral, it is also always a good idea to hold a memorial meeting. Sharing experiences one had of and with the person who has died and thinking of her lovingly reassures and uplifts the departed soul.

If this cannot take place so soon, it should still occur whenever possible, because such loving thoughts light up the spiritual world and act as a balm for the dead person. These are greatly enhanced by uplifting, live (rather than recorded) music, especially singing. This is an occasion also for reciting verses or meditations that the deceased worked with, such as Rudolf Steiner's Foundation Stone Meditation; and for one particular verse which he gave for the dead as follows:

Angels, Archangels and Archai
In the ether weaving,
Receive man's web of destiny.

In Exusiai, Dynamis and Kyriotetes
In the astral feeling of the cosmos,
The just consequences of the earthly life of man
Die into the realm of being.

In Thrones and Cherubim and Seraphim
As their deeds of being,
The justly transmuted fruits of the earthly life of man
Are resurrected.[2]

Memorial meetings can also take place on anniversaries of death days or birthdays.

The memorial meeting is always a very interesting occasion because we discover aspects of the person we did not know. A child's relationship with the deceased is different to that of a work colleague, or sister, and through mutual sharing we can get a real feeling of having actually enhanced our own relationship to the departed, because we can start to have glimpses of how karma wove this soul's web of destiny.

For the living, the memorial meeting can also provide an important opportunity to let go of and transform any negative thoughts and feelings we may have harboured, and to come to terms with any wrongs which we may have done the departed. The dead really experience like a wound both the injustices caused to them and those done by them, and the living are the only ones who can resolve such things. If a dead person's name was wrongly besmirched, we can help her tremendously by clearing it, for otherwise this remains unresolved for the soul in the spiritual world.

It is very important to banish all 'how could you leave me like that' thoughts, because a higher perspective shows that, except in the case of suicide, we die at the right moment in accordance with our karma. Our earthly selves of course feel a great sense of loss, and this is also felt by the departed — they feel our pain and it also upsets them. If we can manage to put on a brave face, both inwardly and outwardly, this strength also helps the departed soul to come to terms with the new situation.

The memorial meeting is very different from the memorial service: the service invokes the spiritual world at a much higher and more intense level. While the deceased experience our loving thoughts like a candle being lit, the memorial service is like the sun coming out for them.

In Chapter 7 we will look further at some of the ways in which we can foster our individual connections to those who have died.

The ashes

In the UK the ashes are usually delivered in a plastic urn by the undertaker, and the question immediately arises of what to do with them. They often sit on the mantlepiece until someone decides what to do; but if we leave them there too long we can start feeling the departed soul's frustration. This is because the ashes are now part of the earth and should return to the earth. Rudolf Steiner indicated that the ashes should be buried in the earth, rather than scattered.[3] The ashes should therefore be buried directly into the soil, or in a biodegradable urn.

If possible ask the dying person where she wants her ashes buried before she dies. We have a much wider choice here than with a burial. Do however be sensitive about the place where the ashes are buried, and hold a short ceremony with the character of a memorial meeting: recite some verses, read from the Bible and the Lord's Prayer, sing a hymn or nice song, for the dead person will be very aware of what is going on and will be part of it. If we choose a site which we do not own, permission may need to be sought from the owner. The ashes need to be in a site which is unlikely to be seriously disturbed (other than normal gardening) for about 30 years. The love you put into keeping the burial place of the ashes beautiful is directly experienced by the dead person.

The grave

Burial entrusts the body to the earth in a slower process than cremation. As with ashes, our physical remains provide important spiritualized substance for the future of the earth.[4] It is appropriate, and appreciated by the departed soul, when friends and loved ones take the time and trouble to tend the grave and make sure it remains beautiful.

For many people, visiting and tending the grave or memorial garden becomes a means of orientating themselves in their love for the departed friend: they can express this love in a physical deed, which the latter directly experiences. All loving thoughts help the departed soul. Beautiful live music or singing can intensify our bond at the graveside or elsewhere. If you are unable to look after the grave yourself, the dead person will be grateful if you can get somebody else to do it.

Grieving

The extent to which you are affected by the death obviously depends on the nature of your relationship with the person who dies: you are bound to suffer grief if it is someone close to you. Grieving is human. While the desire to be stoical is very strong in many people, and admirable, we also have to acknowledge our natural feelings.

The reality is that when someone close to us dies, we

understand it intellectually but do not yet fully grasp the fact. Our habits continue; for instance we may find ourselves putting on the kettle to make tea for the dead person, or expect her to come through the front door at any moment. This unreal stage can last several weeks. In the first few weeks there is a lot of activity — the funeral to arrange and friends to phone up; but when that stops we can feel very alone and bereft. If you feel like talking to a priest, do so: he or she is there for such things, and knows about the process you are going through.

In these circumstances remember that the dead person is indeed still with us, upset that we are upset and having to cope with a completely new situation and environment. Crying is important, is part of the process, and will come suddenly. We have good days and bad days. The letters we receive often bring the reality back in a very vivid way, when we see how other people also experience the loss. Such letters are very important and can be acts of love that are very helpful for the departed soul.

All we can do is live day by day, knowing that grief is part of the human experience. The first time is the most difficult, especially if a child dies; but once we have experienced this process, we know what to expect when it happens again. If we don't cry, and talk to friends about our grief, we may suppress it; and then internalized grief can lead to illness. But if a year passes and we are still crying, it would be good to seek spiritual advice from a priest, or also medical advice from an anthroposophical doctor, homeopath or other trusted professional.

Tranquillizers should definitely be avoided, for they stop the grieving process in its tracks, and therefore prevent us from moving forwards again.

Even years afterwards we may sometimes suddenly find ourselves ambushed by a flood of tears, if someone very close to us has died.

Wherever possible, concentrate on the happy memories, and on what your relationship with the dead person gave you and meant to you. Try to adopt the '3 to 1' rule if you find yourself in a very low state: allowing only one negative thought for 3 positive thoughts. The dead experience what we are thinking. Negative thoughts hinder them in their progress, as well as impeding us too after our own death. Death is only a physical separation. We are karmically linked with those close to us, karma that goes back through many lives and will go on into the future through many lives. Karma takes care of and balances out injustices — so let it take care; and concentrate on what is positive.

During this grieving period it may well be that we have a vision of the dead person, experience a waft of characteristic smell, tobacco or favourite flower, hear her voice, feel a touch on our shoulder. This is to comfort us, so we need not feel fear but just take it as confirmation that the departed soul is with us and knows what is going on. If you feel that the dead person is clinging to you or oppressing you we strongly suggest that you consult a priest. Such things can happen if people cross the threshold with strong materialism in their souls or die by their own hand.

6

INDIVIDUAL DEATH
CIRCUMSTANCES

Like every birth, the time, place and circumstances of every death are unique and individual. As the way we are born influences how our life unfolds on earth, so the circumstances of our death affect the way we cross over into the spiritual world, and the experiences we have in our life after death. Though each death is unique, we also have certain experiences in common with others who have died in a similar way.

Rudolf Steiner spoke many times about the differences between death that comes about by natural causes — illness, old age — and death due to external causes such as accidents and natural catastrophes. He also described the different spiritual circumstances which arise when someone dies young, in the midst of life; or after a long, fulfilled life.

Death in childhood

For parents the death of a child is the most difficult, heart-rending thing to bear. Comfort can really only come through understanding the eternal nature of the human spirit.

A distinction needs to be made between the death of children and adolescents. Younger children have hardly begun to unfold their earthly karma, retaining their prebirth connection with the spiritual world. At death they reconnect with it swiftly, going directly into the realm of the angels, carried there by their guardian angel. In the Christian Community a special funeral service is held for children, which addresses parents' mourning and grief, and encourages a strengthening of faith. From the age of puberty onwards, when individual earthly karma begins, the funeral service is the same as for adults.

When young people die they take back with them much unused life force, which would have been used up in an older person. This means they have a stronger perception of the spiritual world at first, but they also stay very connected to their original family, participating closely in things from the other side. The deceased child remains close to us and accompanies us, whereas *we* accompany the deceased adult.[1] The heavenly presence of the souls of children who have died young radiate susbstantial forces of devotion and reverence into the world.[2]

Death in the prime of life

When someone dies in the prime of life, the intimation of mortality that arises for those left behind has a very sobering effect within the deceased soul's peer group, and the funeral is usually packed with family, friends and colleagues. If the deceased has young children it also raises tremendously practical questions of support for the family, and for young children who have lost a parent.

Young children actually cope more easily with such a death, and understand it better than teenagers. From the adolescent years onwards it can be a very difficult time. The remaining parent, caught up in his own grief, also has to help his grieving children. Godparents and relatives have a real role to play here, both practically and emotionally, especially if the death results in a shortage of money.

The departed one is often as surprised as those he has left, and has to orientate himself in these new circumstances — but will also be very concerned for loved ones who must suddenly fend without him, and will be doing everything possible from beyond the threshold, sending helpful thoughts to inspire and embrace those connected with him.

As in the case of a child, those who die in the prime of life experience the spiritual world in a heightened way. They take with them the unused life forces of the etheric body. Such forces are also ones which the spiritual world needs and can use. However, many people who die when they are fully involved in earthly life have no understanding of what is happening to them, so it is important that they have a proper funeral service, and receive ongoing support and warm, guiding thoughts. The next chapter examines some of the ways to do this.

The death of a loved one who has departed from us in the prime of life may be difficult for us to fathom and come to terms with. Looking at all the circumstances surrounding an individual destiny and death will often enable us, despite the pain we feel, to find an inner thread of order and wisdom in it.

Death due to old age

This is the end of a long process of ageing, in which we graduallly withdraw from the body and physical life. Our life-forces are used up and we have the chance to review our life before we die. Rudolf Steiner describes how the elderly bring a blessing to the earth because, by living a long life, the body is spiritualized.[3] This happens irrespective of the state of consciousness in old age, of whether the person is in possession of his mental faculties; and although circumstances may be subjectively difficult, is an objective blessing for the earth.

In the slow process of excarnation, the so called 'double' or 'doppelganger' — a being that is composed of and bears our lower nature — loosens from us and can therefore be experienced months, weeks or days before death.[4]

This withdrawing of the double can be quite surprising, accompanied by restlessness, uncharacteristic bad language or other strange behaviour. After this however, the person becomes more peaceful. Three days before death the double has to leave the body, and after this a distinct change in the breathing can be observed. This is why doctors usually know when the end is getting close.

For an old person a memorial meeting is a wonderful idea, both because the memory tableau of a long life is very extensive, and also because it helps the living to remember the person as he was in his prime, not just as he was in very old age.

By the age of 72 we have fulfilled our karmic obligations in life, so everything after that occurs more in the realm of free will, even if habits become ingrained. Of course, all our actions continue to create new karma, but there is no longer any karmic necessity. Wisdom can come with old age, and that wisdom is also accessible to us from beyond the threshold after someone has died. The elderly have a special connection with the young and many of us feel that our much older friends, who have crossed the threshold years ago, are now actively helping us. They are now interested in helping us on earth, and can be sources of inspiration, of ideas and will impulses we have if we think over problems and questions with them in mind.[5]

Immediate post-death reading of the gospels in the presence of the body of an old person who has died helps us lift ourselves up to the holy realm where his birth into the spiritual world is taking place.

Death as a result of illness

The predisposition we have towards illness depends very much on the way our soul and life forces interweave with the physical body which has been prepared for us and entrusted to us for this earthly life. Each type of illness presents its own unique challenge.

Illness helps our development and personal evolution. By developing forces of healing from within we take a step forwards on our path, a step closer to becoming truly human. An illness can lead back to health if our bodily organization and forces of destiny can still use and work with what has been newly gained through the illness. An illness will lead to death if a new body is needed to enable the newly won forces to be used. If we die from an illness, new possibilities of using these forces achieved through the illness will be waiting to unfold in the path of life after death.[6]

Death through accident

Death through accident always comes as a great shock to us, an unexpected stroke of destiny that changes our lives from one day to the next. It is always a challenge to a mourning community to support and try to understand and carry such an event with the greatest sensitivity. Much tact is needed to sense how much protection, but also how much presence of others and awareness is needed by the closest relatives and friends who have to cope with such shock and loss.

A priest and others may be able to help deepen understanding of this event. They can accompany the bereaved through the many stages of coming to terms with and accepting what has happened.

Blame is very destructive both for the dead person and us. It is good if we can eradicate all negative feelings and try to foster forgiveness. This is also true for death at anybody else's hand. Karma will eventually resolve and compensate for that. Our job here is to forgive. If the body was destroyed in an accident, for instance in a fire, it is doubly difficult for both the relatives and the deceased,[7] and makes a memorial service and memorial meeting all the more important.

Rudolf Steiner spoke about the relationship of accident to destiny with the following words:

> If you understand that a person may experience deeper layers of consciousness, you will also understand that not only external causes of illness may be sought by man, but also external strokes of fate which he cannot explain rationally, the rationality of which works, however, from deeper strata of consciousness. Thus it is reasonable to suppose that a person would not out of his ordinary consciousness place himself where he may be struck by lightning; with his ordinary consciousness he would do anything to avoid standing where the lightning may strike him. But there may be a consciousness active within him which lies much deeper than ordinary consciousness, and which through foresight not possessed by ordinary consciousness leads him to the very place where lightning may strike him — and wills that he should be so struck. The person really seeks out the accident.[8]

Death through accident is an experience of great importance for the soul entering the world of spirit. It intensifies the moment of transition so strongly that it works on us like a strengthening of our identity, of our ego consciousness. This strengthening of our inner being stays with us when we proceed into the world of spirit, up to the final moment (usually after hundreds of years) when we approach the earth again for a new incarnation. For this reason our higher being, working out of a different consciousness than our daily one, can sometimes guide us into such circumstances.[9]

People who have left earthly life through an accidental or sudden death (for instance in times of war) become part of a greater, wonderful mission in the world of the spirit. They have had to sacrifice the forces of their etheric and astral bodies and ego, which could have supported and carried the physical body for many years. Lives which end suddenly in this way cannot fulfil their possibilities. Instead such possibilities are carried back as impulses and forces into the world of spirit. Drawing on the treasures of these unused possibilities, such souls become messengers in the world of spirit. Rudolf Steiner compares early-departed souls with people who have idealism on earth and who are therefore able to lift the quality of life on earth beyond materialism. They meet other souls there, especially souls on their way down to the earth and — through the fact that their lives on earth were not fully lived out — are able to show them that mankind can still find high ideals in earth existence, that life on earth still contains the spiritual as something precious.[10]

Violent death

Death through violence always comes as a deep shock to all of us. A lot of support is needed to be able to go through this very difficult experience. Such a death is always very tragic, not least because it can also involve a police investigation and there may be unresolved questions about what really happened.

In such circumstances the victim's experience is that his life on earth has been taken away by the will of another person. The late Rev. Evelyn Capel recommended in these circumstances that the bereaved should pray that the victim may look upon what is happening to him with the eyes of Christ because suffering will be still greater if the soul harbours impulses of hate or revenge. If the soul realizes how helpless perpetrators are in the grip of evil impulses, feelings of compassion can console him, especially if he can find the help and courage of Christ to face the powers which have attacked him. Still deeper, in the heart of Christ, he will find powers that transform his grim experience into powers of soul that can be used for creating what is good.

Prayers calling on the healing power of Christ and the reading of the story of the crucifixion from St Luke's Gospel help, for the words of Christ spoken from the cross are deeds of transformation.

A soul who dies in this way will need much ongoing thought and prayers as a protection for the difficult circumstances he finds himself thrown into. If the person who has died in this way did not have strong spiritual inclinations, reading to him will be particularly important (see Chapter 7). This will help him understand his new situation, and should go on for a long time — years, rather than days. Also a community or congregation can help by joining forces, and the services in the Christian Community can build a gateway for such a soul to find orientation and access to the divine.

Someone who has died through violence will not be ready or prepared for entering the spiritual world, and will feel a great longing for his physical body. Therefore it is better not to cremate a person who has been killed but bury him, so that the departed soul will still have this point of orientation on earth. A priest will be able to accompany such a situation over a longer period, and ask the congregation to help with their prayers.

Suicide

Although suicide is a breach of divine law, the spiritual world makes provision for it, and it is not true to say that suicides are simply outcasts in the spiritual world! Yet because the suicide's astral body is unprepared for death, he continues to long for his physical body for as long as he would have lived on earth. Suicides therefore have to stay in the sphere of the earth until they would have died in accordance with their pre-birth karmic plan. Through this experience they gain understanding that life is valuable, meaningful and purposeful, and that we should not simply throw it away. They will carry such understanding into their next life on earth.

Rudolf Steiner described how such a soul has a great longing for his physical body.[11] It will be helpful for the departed soul if he can orientate himself through and towards his body. For this reason those who die in this way should be buried rather than cremated.

Suggestions contained in Chapter 7 for maintaining links with those who have died need to be treated with caution in the case of suicides, for they have a lot of energy and disturbance, and it is not a straightforward matter if the person was close to you. It can be a help in these circumstances not to think directly of the suicide but to pray to Christ, also asking your guardian angel to convey and support the soul, and carry such support to the suicide's guardian angel. If you feel that the soul of the suicide is very close, pray for Christ's protection so that your own personal energy fields are not disturbed by him.

It is actually too much for one person without experience in this realm to take on helping a suicide. It really requires a community of people, because the suicide tends to cling to the people he loved on earth. If you are on your own it would be best to go regularly to church and bring the suicide into your prayers within the church service, but to watch very carefully for any changes which take place in your own soul or body — and if they do, consult a priest. This is a difficult area, and it is best to talk to someone with experience of it. Any supporting work or activity needs to continue over an extended period.

Life support machines, organ transplants, euthanasia

To summarize some of the thoughts expressed in this book, we could say that death is a moment of real meeting of the world of temporal matter with the world of eternal spirit. Just as the heavenly aspect of our birth finds its reflection in the birth horoscope, so the death horoscope gives our moment of death its unique significance.

Through developments in modern medicine and technology, prolonging life has become possible in some circumstances. We could all find ourselves in the situation of having to decide whether to attempt to prolong life through the use of life support machines or through organ transplantation. Such a situation throws up many complex ethical and medical considerations. The following paragraphs can only be seen as a very brief airing of some considerations which may be involved. In each specific situation further professional advice will certainly be needed. In attempting to reach a decision in each case, we need to seek objective spiritual criteria.

In facing the prospect of an organ transplant we must consider some profound spiritual realities, including the fact that the required organ will probably have been removed before another's clinical death has occurred. The usual time for the removal of the organ is after brain death has been ascertained but before death in its complete finality has come about (clinical death). This operation has to be performed at this early stage to ensure that the organ in question is still filled with vitality and can therefore properly serve the person in need of it. The transplant organ is considered by the body receiving it to be 'foreign matter', and hence medication will be needed to suppress the immune system and to help prevent the body from rejecting the new organ.

No two human bodies are the same. Our physical body is individually designed and fashioned with the help of the hierarchies to provide a fit dwelling place for our unique, eternal individuality.[12] The bodily organs have a unique spiritual purpose in supporting our life on earth.

What does it mean to have an intimate and vital organ formed for a different human body now transplanted into our own body? What does it mean for our remaining life on earth? What does it mean for life after death? What does it mean for the person who has donated the organ? These questions could form part of the criteria for a decision about whether to accept or decline an organ transplant. Each case must be considered separately, and there are no easy answers.

While the use of life support machines and organ transplantation gives us the possibility of prolonging life, questions relating to the wilful curtailing of life, of euthanasia, are increasingly debated. Above all we can consider whether, ultimately, euthanasia is any different from suicide.

THE BRIDGE BETWEEN THE LIVING AND THE DEAD

The first three days after death are a profound time in which the soul and spirit slowly withdraw from the body, an intense time of farewell. Through our presence and thoughts we can try to support and accompany this holy process.

At the end of this first period the funeral will usually be held, and the journey of the soul into the heights of the spiritual world begins—a long journey with many different stages. Some of the books listed on p. 71 contain detailed accounts of this journey after death.

The journey into life after death, once the etheric body has dissolved, begins with several years spent in the astral world, going through what is known as *kama loca*. All souls experience this, apart from young children, whether their lives were longer or shorter. During this period we relive all the details of our lives backwards, starting from the moment of death and going back to birth. Typically this experience lasts about one third of our earthy life. We experience vividly our effect on others for good or ill, and whether our words and actions wove or tore the fabric of humanity as a whole.

Our feelings in this astral realm are far more intense than they were in earthly life. This is a very humbling experience and is only bearable because we are permeated through and through by divine love. The guidance of the spiritual hierarchies (from guardian angels right up to the seraphim) enables the first seeds of our future destiny to be sown, in the form of a longing to serve the good and redeem the bad.

During this period we also have to sever our connections with the material earth, and release the tastes and habits which we acquired during our lives and for which we need a physical body. One friend who liked eating and talking imagined that for him this would be comparable to attending a lively dinner party with no mouth! Soon after death the departed start to miss the people they were connected to during life, and will try to be near them. Many people have this experience – and they are right. The dead simply want to be with those they loved while on earth. As time goes on – and each person is individual in this respect – the departed soul starts to lose the very close connection with the earth, and begins to find access to the higher levels of the astral world. Friends can sometimes sense that the departed soul, though further on in this spiritual journey, is still just as close to them. The dead do not forget us, it is usually we who forget them.

Keeping the dead in our thoughts is very important for them. Obviously the kinds of thoughts which are filled with personal egotism are not helpful. Loving thoughts are especially helpful, but simply thinking about the one who has died is also directly felt and appreciated.

The dead live at first in the astral sphere, that of our thoughts and feelings, and there have the ability to perceive what we are thinking and feeling. They can read our thoughts and also permeate our feelings. In other words they are in a very different environment from that of earth and have to get accustomed to it. Their ability to explore and progress in their new environment depends in part on knowing what is there, in having either prepared for it in life, by having studied spiritual science, or through receiving guidance from those on earth who relate to the spiritual world in thought and prayer.

To summarize, the dead still feel their connections to earth, and are trying to understand their new surroundings while at the same time undergoing intense soul experiences of the life review, and loss of the physical body. For those who have taken their own lives, different laws apply (see Chapter 6).

Simply thinking of the dead frequently helps them to remain with us, and is a blessing to them. Having photographs of one's dead friends also helps make them present to us.

Our loving thoughts of the dead ease their soul experience: thinking with warmth and affection of them now in the spiritual world, or of things we did together, all the good experiences we shared. Try to ensure these memories are largely positive, because any negativity is sensed by the dead as small acts of hate, which they feel acutely in their new landscape of abounding love.

Simply sending thoughts is not always enough for the dead person to receive them immediately. Lighting a candle, eurythmy, uplifting live music, or singing can intensify our inner connection to the departed soul. Likewise we can think of our dead friends when hearing live music, watching eurythmy, or singing or playing music ourselves, inviting them to be with us. At night, when we are asleep, we are in the same realm as the dead and they surround us, so thoughts we have about them during the day will certainly reach them then. Just as we need daily physical nourishment, so too the so-called dead seek spiritual nourishment which they are able to find when our thoughts and prayers turn to them. Our spirit-filled thoughts help to create spiritual cornfields which nourish the dead.[1]

Rudolf Steiner often mentioned how supportive it is to read content from spiritual science to the dead. This reading of serious spiritual literature helps them orientate themselves in their new situation, clarifying spirit light for them, enabling them to understand more of their new environment.

Reading for the dead starts after the funeral, and from then on it is something we should continue with. Whenever you read a lecture by Rudolf Steiner or a piece of spiritually significant literature think of your dead friends and include them. This helps them as they can perceive our thought forms. Reading can be done aloud or silently. What is important is clear thought; and as a general principle we should read only what we can take in ourselves. If you fall asleep inwardly as you 'read' it does not work, although of course the dead still experience your efforts and love on their behalf, and that in itself is comforting to them.

Deceased souls are actually fully occupied in the spiritual world, and have plenty to do, so it is best to read for them on a regular basis, daily or weekly, preferably at the same day or time on each occasion. In this way you develop a rhythm that supports the whole activity.

A further possibility of connecting with those who have died is by bearing the dead person in mind when attending a church service, concert or lecture.

If you start working with the dead intensively, do this as far as possible through your connection to Christ who is the true door to the realm of the dead. The Christian Community's Act of Consecration of Man consciously addresses and includes the dead through Christ within its service.

Rudolf Steiner gave many verses for accompanying the dead, but here is one that covers many aspects that have been described. The last three lines of this verse bring to expression something of the soul's experience in kama loca, of its need to find orientation in the spiritual world, and the longing to remain connected with us on earth:

> Faithfully
> I will follow your soul
> Through the gate of death
> Into the light-engendering
> Time places
> With love I will ease spirit coldness for you
> With knowing I will untangle spirit light for you
> With thinking I will linger with you.[2]

If we can set time aside to turn to the dead on a regular basis, imagining them with us, we do a deed of charity which goes far beyond our earthly understanding, and is of immeasurable grace to those whom we love on the other side. If we do it regularly the dead learn to draw near to us at that time.

The dead help us tremendously. They live in the soul-spirit world where we are when asleep. They surround us at that time and we are in constant night-time communication, although we rarely remember it. These were our friends on earth who still love us, and they now live in the realm of world thoughts, where all the wisdom of the world is contained. After the soul has passed out of kama loca, the astral world, into devachan or the heavenly world, this wisdom is of course still greater. The dead help by inspiring us, they think *in* us all the time and many of our best ideas are direct inspirations from them. If we learn to pay attention we can distinguish the different qualities and origins of many of our thoughts. As a general principle, thoughts you wake up with in the morning are often connected with the dead.

Rudolf Steiner encapsulates this beautifully once more in the following two verses, where the dead speak from beyond the threshold.

No boundaries separate
where spirit links sustain
light-brilliant,
love-radiant
eternal soul bonds.

So I am in your thoughts,
so you in mine.[3]

I was united with you;
remain united within me.

We will converse
in the speech of eternal being.
We will be active
where deeds take effect,
we will weave in spirit
where human thoughts are woven
in the word of eternal thoughts.[4]

APPENDIX

PRACTICAL ASPECTS

Laying out the body

1. In the UK there is no need to call the undertaker immediately after someone has died.
2. In the UK the death must be registered with the local registrar of births, marriages and deaths within five days.
3. Among the first to be contacted should be the priest and the doctor.
4. In normal circumstances in the UK you can keep the body at home or a chapel of rest, unless a post mortem is required.
5. Two or three people are required to help prepare the body for laying out, one of whom needs some knowledge of what it entails.
6. Generally speaking it is a simple exercise and one you should not be scared of.
7. If there are nurses available, they will normally do this as a matter of course, but if the death occurs elsewhere this is often left to the undertaker. It is up to you what you do, however, and if there is a friend or a local funeral support group or a nurse available, they will be able to assist.
8. If a white shroud is not available, then a (white) blouse or similar may be an alternative.
9. Lay some flowers on the body, light one or two candles.

10. Provide a Bible from which those who come to say their farewells can read.
11. Keep the environment cool.
12. It is preferable that the body is not embalmed (as this hampers the soul's progress). You will need to instruct the undertaker not to embalm.

Legal requirements following death (applicable in the UK)

1. In the UK the medical doctor confirms the death, and the Registry of Births, Marriages and Deaths in the area where the person died issues a formal death certificate. Usually an appointments system is operated. The registrar also issues the undertaker with a certificate for disposal of the body.
2. The undertaker requires the death certificate but needs an additional doctor's certification if the body is to be cremated. The undertaker can organize this if no other doctor is available, and this fee will be added to the cost. You can of course organize it yourself
3. If the deceased person was not under medical supervision when he died, or there are suspicious circumstances, the doctor may be unwilling to issue his certificate and there may be the need for a post-mortem or an inquest. Normally the GP can deal with this by talking to the Coroner, and if the Coroner is happy the GP will issue his certificate.
4. If the Coroner wants to investigate the body to find the cause of death, there may often be a waiting time,

so some time will elapse before the funeral can be held. In these circumstances, consult the priest about what best to do.

5. Be aware that if somebody leaves their body to medical research (which we do not recommend) the hospital may well have finished with it six months later, so that you can have it back for disposal. Most people believe that by bequeathing your body in this way you avoid the cost of a funeral! But this is not necessarily so. You really need to think this through clearly in the light of other aspects highlighted in this book.

Frequently asked questions

(The answers apply to regulations in England and Wales)

Q Who arranges the funeral?

A The executor named in the will, or in the absence of a will the next of kin.

Q How do I make sure I have the funeral I want?

A Include your instructions in the will and state on the outside of the envelope that it includes funeral instructions. The best idea is to tell the priest in person and in writing but also make sure your relevant relatives/friends know your wishes, so they follow them when the time comes. Relatives can have very odd ideas at moments of grief, so be really quite specific about whom you wish to invite, flowers (nothing is more miserable than a flowerless funeral), and remember that relatives are not experienced funeral arrangers.

As a checklist:

- In which church would you like your funeral service held?
- Who do you want to organize the funeral?
- Burial/cremation?
- Who will be invited (make sure someone knows who your friends are)?
- What flowers/donations to which charity?
- Where do you want the ashes buried and who is to organize it?

Q Who pays for it?

A The funeral is paid for out of the estate of the deceased. If the deceased had no money, and there is nobody to pay for it, speak to the social security office before doing anything.

Q How do I make a will?

A A solicitor is the most reliable way, but there are also professional will writers. In each case find out the fee in advance. Alternatively, you can get a will form from good stationery shops, but remember you must follow the signing and witnessing rules, otherwise it is invalid.

Q What happens if I don't make a will?

A All your assets pass to the next of kin in accordance with legal provision in absence of a will. If you have neither spouse, children or known relatives YOU

MUST MAKE A WILL, otherwise your money will go to the government.

Q Does the will have to be written?

A Yes. It must be in writing and properly witnessed.

Q What do I do with it when I've executed it?

A You must keep it in a safe place which would be obvious to someone looking for it, or give it to someone you trust. Do not give it to a person who is not a beneficiary but would inherit if the will were lost. If in doubt, the bank is a good place to keep it.

Q If I am executor, what do I do with the will when the person has died?

A You have to take out a grant of probate. These days it is a streamlined procedure in the UK: you phone the local probate registry and they send you the forms which you fill in and send back. They call you for interview four weeks later and give you the probate, which is your authority to deal with the assets. Alternatively, take the will to a solicitor (more appropriate for bigger or more complicated cases).

Q What if there is no will?

A Follow the same procedure as above but ask for the 'letters of administration'. You have to prove you are the closest relation to the deceased. So if it is your uncle who has died, and he has children, they would naturally be expected to do the job.

Q   What if the will has been lost?

A   It is presumed that a lost will was destroyed by the person who made it as he changed his mind. If the will is lost, it is disregarded, and assets pass to those people who would inherit if no will was made.

NOTES

'GA' refers to the collected edition of the works of Rudolf Steiner as published in the original German. The dates given refer to the day on which Rudolf Steiner gave the relevant lecture. Where lectures have been translated and published in English, the relevant volume is shown. Publication details appear in the Bibliography (see p. 71). In cases where lectures are not available in published form, typescripts are often available from the Rudolf Steiner Library, 35 Park Road, London NW1 6XT.

Chapter 1
[1] See Rudolf Steiner, *Theosophy*.

Chapter 2
[1] GA 261: Berlin, 30 October 1910.
[2] GA 181: Berlin, 5 February 1918. English translation in *Life Beyond Death*.
[3] GA 261: Reinach, 22 September 1918.
[4] GA 261: Arlesheim, 14 January 1919.
[5] Dornach, 8 October 1921.
[6] Dornach, 8 October 1921.
[7] Stuttgart, 12 July 1923.
[8] Ibid.
[9] GA 236, Dornach, 27 June 1924. English translation in *Karmic Relationships*, Vol. II.

Chapter 3
[1] Matthew 6, v.5ff.

Chapter 4
[1] GA 161, Dornach, 2 February 1915.
[2] I Peter 3,19; Ephesians 4,9; Romans 14,9.

3 Verses by Steiner usually address the situation which begins after the first three days. During the first three days after death the dead are involved in the mighty panorama of their lives.

4 GA 94, Leipzig, 30 June 1906.

Chapter 5

1 From the Creed of the Christian Community.

2 GA 237, Dornach, 4 July 1924. English translation in *Karmic Relationships*, Vol. III.

3 From a conversation with Ilona Schubert.

4 GA 294, Stuttgart, 23 August 1919. English translation in *Study of Man*.

Chapter 6

1 GA 174a, Munich, 14 February 1918. English translation in *The Mission of the Archangel Michael*.

2 GA 181, Berlin, 5 February 1918. English translation in *Life Beyond Death*.

3 GA 183, Dornach, 2 September 1918.

4 GA 178, St. Gallen, 16 November 1917.
  GA 147, Munich, 30 August 1913.

5 GA 168, Zurich, 3 September 1916.

6 GA 120, Hamburg, 19 May 1910. English translation in *Manifestations of Karma*.

7 This is because he cannot gain orientation from seeing his body, unlike most other post-death circumstances.

8 GA 120, Hamburg, 21 May 1920. English translation in *Manifestations of Karma*.

9 GA 168, Zurich, 24 October 1916.

10 GA 157, Berlin, 20 November 1915. English translation in *Destines of Individuals and of Nations*.

11 GA 93a, Berlin, 7 October 1905. English translation in *Foundations of Esotericism*.

¹² GA 231, The Hague, 17 November 1923. English translation in *Supersensible Man*.

Chapter 7

¹ GA 140, Bergen, 10 October 1913. English translation in *Life Beyond Death*.
² GA 261, for Gertrud Noss. Translation by Christopher Bamford.
³ *Living With the Dead*, Rudolf Steiner Press 2002. Translation by Matthew Barton.
⁴ Ibid.

BIBLIOGRAPHY

By Rudolf Steiner:

Destinies of Individuals and Nations, Rudolf Steiner Press 1987

Foundations of Esotericism, Rudolf Steiner Press 1983

Inner Nature of Man, Rudolf Steiner Press 1994

Karmic Relationships Vol. II, Rudolf Steiner Press 1997

Karmic Relationships Vol. III, Rudolf Steiner Press 2002

Life Beyond Death, Rudolf Steiner Press 1995

Life Between Death and Rebirth, Anthroposophic Press 1968

Living with the Dead (Meditations), Rudolf Steiner Press 2002

Archangel Michael, His Mission and Ours, Anthroposophic Press 1994

Manifestations of Karma, Rudolf Steiner Press 2000

Staying Connected, Anthroposophic Press 1999

Supersensible Man, Anthroposophic Press 1961

Theosophy, Anthroposophic Press 1994

Verses and Meditations, Rudolf Steiner Press 1993

By other authors:

Stanley Drake, *Though You Die*, Floris Books 2002

Karin von Schilling, *Where Are You? Coming to Terms With the Death of My Child*, Anthroposophic Press, 1988